eat drink grow

by Susan Baker

illustrated by Joanna Stubbs

MACDONALD
3 4 5

'I'm hungry. Can I have some crisps?'
'Not now, it's nearly time for lunch,'
said Mummy.
'Can you find some orange juice on the shelf?'

'I don't want my lunch.
I like crisps best.
Why can't I eat crisps all the time?'
'You need different kinds of food
to help you grow and give you energy
for running about, just like a car needs petrol
to make it go,' said Mummy.

'I'm going to finish first,
then I can go out to play.'
'Slow down, don't gobble
or you might choke,' said Daddy.
'Chew your food properly,
that's what your teeth are for.'

'Where does my food go inside me?' I asked.
'It goes down a tube to your stomach,
where it gets all churned up
until it is mushy. Then it can be squeezed
along the very, very long tube
that is curled up in your tummy.'

'As the food goes down the long tube,
all the good things go into your blood.
Your heart pumps blood all round your body,
so the good things can be used
to build new skin, bones and muscles.'

'After your body has taken
the good things it needs out of the food,
the rest is squeezed along
to the end of the tube in your bottom.
It comes out as faeces,
when you go to the lavatory.'

'Even though your skin feels dry,
your body has lots of water in it.
Every day your body needs fresh water
to keep it working properly.
Some of the water is turned into urine.
It drips into a stretchy bag
called the bladder.
When it is full, it makes you feel
that you need to go to the lavatory.
The urine takes unwanted things
out of the body with it when you pee.'

'Can I have another drink of water?
I'm very hot.'
'Yes,' said Daddy.
'You have to drink a lot when you're hot,
because some of the water in your body
escapes through your skin as sweat,
to cool you down.
Sometimes you can feel the watery drops
on your forehead.'

'When you are ill,
your body doesn't work very well
and your stomach might try
to empty out the wrong way.
It sends the mushy food up instead of down
and then you are sick.'

'Children need food to help them grow up
but everyone needs food
even if they have finished growing.
Although we can't see it,
our bodies wear out a little bit every day.
If you fall over, you can see how your skin
grows until the graze has healed.'

'Can you see me growing?' I asked.
'Not quite,' said Mummy, 'because it happens
very, very slowly all the time,
even when you are asleep.
You are breathing, digesting
and growing, all the time.'

Notes

Food and drink are often the topic of conversation with young children, which is not surprising when so much time is spent shopping, helping in the kitchen and eating together at table.

Inevitably, arguments will arise over how much and what sort of food should be eaten, especially when members of the family have different tastes. It is difficult to prevent children adding salt and sugar to their food, if they see us doing it.

You can explain that the wide variety of food we eat contains different things that the body needs in order to grow up strong and healthy. Meat, fish, eggs, cheese, peas and beans are all good body-building foods, because they contain protein. We get energy from carbohydrates and fats which can be found in bread, potatoes, yams, egg yolk, meat and fish. Most foods contain vitamins. These are important to keep you healthy. Refined sugar is only good for instant energy, there is no other goodness in it. We should make every effort to discourage a sweet tooth because of the damage it does to teeth.

Young children are often just as interested in what comes out as what goes in, especially during potty training. The workings of the bowels are fairly straightforward: what goes in one end and is not used, comes out the other. The kidneys are more complicated. Young children only need to know that excess fluid is turned into urine by the kidneys and that urine carries out other waste products with it.

Most families have their own family words for urine, faeces and lavatory, and parents might prefer to substitute these in the text when they first read the book aloud.

© Macdonald & Co (Publishers) Ltd 1984

First published 1984 by
Macdonald & Co (Publishers) Ltd
Maxwell House, Worship Street
London EC2A 2EN
Member of BPCC plc

ISBN 0 356 09958 X

Consultants: Dr Iona Heath
Michele Ehrenmark
Editor: Lucille Powney
Art Agency: B. L. Kearley Ltd
Production: Rosemary Bishop

Printed and bound in Great Britain by Purnell & Sons (Book Production) Ltd.
Member of the BPCC Group, Paulton, Bristol.